"If we surrendered

to earth's intelligence

we could rise up rooted,

   like trees"

Rainer Maria Rilke

"How Surely Gravity's Law."

JACKIE MORRIS
FEATHER, LEAF, BARK & STONE

unbound

For Peter Florence
and Becky Shaw
with love.

To gather thoughts,
shape thoughts to words,
type words onto leaf.

Each sheet becomes its own island.
Some are peninsulas.

At the edge of the land
where the rock meets the sea,
I found them.

Stored in a book,
bound with a cord,
brought to the light,
as time passed
each image was captured.

The day began with low cloud,
sky coloured like a wagtail's breast.
After days of high winds, calm.
Insects rested on the golden sheets,
read the words with their tongues.

Listening to the soundscape
as each piece lay
on white paper, waiting,
for focus, and sometimes the wind
sang through the grass,
through blackthorn branches,
lifting the tissue of gold,
not snatching, just holding.
And the house and the hedgebank
gave shelter.

And the birds in the hedge
added voices;
the sharp song of wren,
the call of the blackbirds,
while overhead flocks of rooks
conversed, and raven flew and
the song of the air in their wings
formed a part of the making
of image, not taking,
just seeking a way to share.

There was a peace in the turning
of pages, of lifting each sheet,
as light gently shifted
with each passing second.

For light and time are a river,
constant in motion,
and things always change.

51° 52' 56.19" N
5° 16' 7.98" W   30.45m (99.9ft)

By feather, leaf, bark & stone

Shaped by tide's turn, smooth, round

By feather, leaf, bark & stone

In sap that flows from root to crown

By feather, leaf, bark & stone

A leaf in water where otters swim

By feather, leaf, bark & stone

Song of raven, the curlew's hymn

There is a web that wraps
around the world,
a tangled place, so easy to
become lost. But look to
the light and you will find
a guide to take you always
by the hand, and lead you
to beauty by perfect paths.

Across the bay,

    a handfull of curlew

        rise, and call,

a mourning song,

    wild -

        echoing

          over

           calm

             sea.

Thoughts,

      often fleeting,

swift as hares,

      caught and held

as language,

      in ink,

to share.

Things to do:
Take a stone for a walk.
Take leaves of gold up hill,
release into the wild.
Take leaves of gold to stream,
place in water, watch light,
bring home, dry.
Find the silence in which to
catch the shape of words.
Breathe, and in between, peace.

How the light comes

                each new day,

on the voices of birds,

        as if their song

is the key to

        the world's turning.

51°53' 27.492"N
5°17' 58.332"W

Wren is a handful of song,

thrown through thorns

splintered feathers

reforming

to form

sweet briar

song at sunrise.

Through dappled light

of early morning sun slant

the fresh fledged

children of

wrens

find first

flights.

To see them,

rise before dawn,

when earth is iron-hard,

water a skin of splinters.

Go to a place where

strips of ancient forest

divide and shelter fields.

Wait.

Here, where the moon

holds the land in monochrome,

owl carries silence,

one by one they rise,

as if out of the earth,

from shallow forms,

or ghost from shelter of trees

to shake frost from fur.

Now hares' breath

joins with fog,

and they run,

to wake their wild blood,

even as the world wakes,

sparks of colour dancing

to a chorus of rook

and the song of wrens.

51° 53'   32. 538" N.
5° 17'   50 37" W.

Never forget

even in darkness

somewhere

small birds

are flying

Redwings:

To hear them, wake at night

when sound is stripped away

by the focus of darkness -

overhead they fly,

navigating by stars and scent,

calling in pin sharp whistles,

And the bird knows

                as it flies,

the piece of the sky

                it inhabits,

that piece is

                always its home.

Far from the sea, where trees
reach down
              to touch the river's
skin,
       where light flows with water,
where twigs
                snag
                     leaf-litter dams,
   on a rock, dark,
                     soft with moss.
Clear water,
             shallow,
                      and riverbed
   all
      small, smoothed stones.

To move through city streets
navigate by trees.
Touch their bark-skin
to hear through fingers how,
beneath concrete
roots connect.
Feel how memory of forest
threads through
each green leaf.

Lat 57°53' 32.622" N
5° 17' 51.402" W

Her leaves give music to wind,
shade in summer,
shelter to small lives,
bird, insect, bat.
On her bark-skin hollows,
scars, give testament to

storms weathered, long life.
Her branches pleach and plait
to reach the light.
At her feet
her scattered children thrive.

My soul is restless with all the
conversations we will never have.
I calm it with ink
        listen to your voice as
    you sing in the past, and dwell
on the space between a breath and
a breath.

        Your life was a grace note
and stories were your blood and
                        bone.

Between a breath and
                a breath
  they fell in love, she was
born, it rained, she grew,
they danced, snow fell,
time stood still, darkness
fell, a bird sang, a heart
  broke.

And how grief is a curious creature that stalks the heart, and the mind. Textured with memory, regret, loss, all the questions never asked, all the time never shared. No longer any possibility for change. It becomes a lesson, to make of each moment the most, to hold each heart gently.

Hard by the wrackline

Close by a tangle

                of feathers

that once had been a

                    bird,

on a slab of dark stone.

A wish.
Not to share the form of a hare,
two hearts beating, one body—
but to slip shape,
become wild on the earth,
Woodcat, pilgrim,
stars for a ceiling,

moss for a bed.

51° 53'   24·462" N
5° 17'   58.812" W.

A True Story

in four parts.

On her wedding day she

danced so fast, so wild,

her veil snagged and tore,

caught on the thorns of

briar,

rose,

bramble.

Her mother took the veil,

mended the lace,

weaving, winding and binding

spells into the patterns,

    with bobbins,

      with pins

        and with love.

Next day she found it,

flawless, like new,

held it high to the sun,

as patterns danced

across her face

and

only then did she see

how the lace had been

mended, with fine filament

strands of her own mother's

beautiful,

long

white

hair.

51° 53' 26.22"N
5° 17' 58.68" W

Whitesands.

The sight of them

a gift from the wild.

On the edge of the wind,

first martins,

then swallow,

then swifts.

A moment, then gone,

leaving memory holding

the shape of wings.

Sea smooth
patterned by time
written on stone,
on a rock where
ravens rest,
textured by lichen,
face turned to the
wide sky

In leaf-light and birdsong
a moment of peace. Secret
lives dwell in shadow. High
on the ridge, a sharp call.
The child of a tawny owl
watches. The earth is rich
with green life and the
peace of the wild.

Things the wind does;
In spring, soft, gentle, often
with rain. Also fierce,
shattering blossom.
Summer, carrying the memory
of desert heat, heavy with
the texture of jasmine,honey_
suckle, rose, heather.

Between hedges,

edges that mark boundaries of

old ways,

paths worn by centuries of

footfall and hoof,

hawthorn twists in wind-woven

branches to hold stone

and red berries.

A storm rises.

There are days,

       unsteady days when

it would seem the earth beneath

feet does shift and roll,

and all seems unsteady

       uncertain.

But I wake to a message from

my child, and an image of a whale
child. This is the shape of hope.

Listen.

In the still air,

to the soft hush of it. Barely

enough weight to move a leaf,

but still, rain.

Turn face to sky, feel it fall,

gentle onto skin.

When does mist become rain?

51° 53' 10.02" N
5° 13' 13.098" W
    altitude. 82·96m (272·19ft)
Airfield

Still air

sky a bowl of blue

and nearby

a single lark lifts,

airborne

on song

then a flock

an exultation

all around

they stand in air

and now even

the grass is singing

hold these birds

in ears

in eyes

as they hold air and

surround the heart

with wild music

Lat – 51°53' 31.872" N
Long – 5°17' 52.698" W
1 Jan 2021.

To watch a barnowl is
to see silence in motion.

Face pale as meadowsweet,

claws sharp as gorse,

wisdom old as oak,

she holds the twilight,

 dancing her hunting

in hushwinged grace.

Fresh water, threads through
reed bed to pool and tumble
over sea-smooth stones.
The sky is a ceiling of
fish-belly silvered cloud,

and a handful of curlew fly,
song falling to touch salt sea.

Peace can be found, always,

between the notes of their song.

Wild Music no1:

The wood, in winter,

beech, birch and oak,

and a song of the wind

caught in the trees,

at the edge of a gale,

ahead of the storm.

A pause -

a space,

between

the notes

of music,

and how it speaks to silence

and becomes the very heart

of all things.

First I saw
rose from ground
smooth movement
catching time to
a stand-still,
leapt wall
wind-swift, foot-sure,
born of the earth,
leaving me rooted.

In quiet ruin, on glossy cranesbill,

English stonecrop, moss,

dark stone and gold rest.

Once a storehouse for bombs,

now tumbled walls tangle

with blackberry bushes.

Now dragonflies and owls hunt

over bullrush and sedge and

  snipe find shelter, sanctuary.

One thousand years folds

to a moment

as the ink dark moon

floods my mind with

its quiet wisdom.

I wonder, had we met,

might we have become friends?

Where runways crumble
and the memory of field
patterns is lost to time,
where flowers draw new
pathways, cover the land
like tapestries, skylarks
rise into the air that
once was loud with the sound
of war.

Ragged buzzard turns

    to face the wind,

opens wings wide,

falls into air that lifts

bird into flight.

    A common act

        of wild faith.

Stormcock,

       mistlethrush,

common bird of youth.

A solitary voice

in the waiting garden,

sings of the storm to come.

Where stones lean in to whisper,
Where fox barks, dragonflies
dance and rain falls

summer-soft on green leaf.
Step by step
to the centre
to leave sea-stone,
gilded,
a map of heart and home.

Hare, fast-fleeting,

time frozen, she rose,

up from the earth

in smooth movement,

over stone wall, away.

Gold burned leaping

silhouette on memory,

making sense of the seeing.

Larks lift,

rise from the skin of the

earth, wings lifting up,

even as the song falls

to my ears where I stand,

earth-bound,

tethered to ground.

Fragile and weathered,

Torn by time and grief,

life seems different.

Splintered, fractured,

ripped, and gathered.

Life becomes storm weathering

to the edges.

Grief, in four parts.

1

I can paint, write,

through almost any circumstance,

anywhere, but, for now,

I cannot find the words I need.

Elusive, they hide, brain

fractured, head, heart, out of

line.

2

Now I understand the phrase
'enduring love',
as I face the chasm that
opens with the loss
of a life,
of two.
How to endure the coming days?

Look

    to the skies,

    to the shape of

            birds,

wing-flash,

       wild song.

wait, quietly,

      the coming of bluebells.

Be glad that,

              years ago,

you chose to live

              on the edge,

where the land

              meets the sea.

Await the coming of swallows,

Hope lifted on dark wings.

51°53' 29.442"N
5°17' 54.75"W

Beneath the dark,

hare hunkers, fragile frame

folded into form,

thistle-down fur holding

day's warmth, crouched

on the skin of the earth,

dreaming the light of

the moon.

Like the Snow Queen's mirror

I feel crackle-glazed

as if

one tap could

shatter me into

a thousand shining splinters

that would

fall to earth.

How,

    when the gale blows

so fierce to shake

the stones of the house,

bending branches to the earth,

denying birds their flight,

it feels that this has always

                    been,

  this rage, this storm, this power.

Then, silence.

                    Stillness follows.

Each leaf waiting.

Not a breath

                    of wind.

And the song of birds

            carries through the calm.

Given into the open hand
of a small child.
Carried along the thread
of a cliff path.

Tucked beneath a lichen covered
rock, half hidden, secret,
beside the sea,
on a blue sky day.

Seen in winter;
ink-dark legs,
coat of rust-red,
walking in sunshine,
nonchalant. Wild thing,
caught out of time,
seen for a moment,
bright against green,
then gone.

Seen in summer;
crossing a field of
long grass and flowers.
A spark of wild,
burnt into the mind's eye,
over the hedge and away,
leaving her tracks
in mind, memory
and heart.

Shaped by tide's turn, smooth, round

By feather, leaf, bark & stone

In sap that flows from root to crown

By feather, leaf, bark & stone

A leaf in water where otters swim

By feather, leaf, bark & stone

Song of raven, the curlew's hymn

By feather, leaf, bark & stone

I thought grief would just
come, but it moves, like the sea,
sometimes calm, reflective,
sometimes in the teeth of
a storm,
far from the shore, floundering.

Two ravens cross the clear blue,
calling, circle the garden,
turn back to the hill.
I let their song call me home.

Listen.

Lark lifts,

light holding feather,

song supporting the weight

of a bird.

Muscle, feather, hollowed

bone - all song.

No space between the notes.

Smoothed,
        rock curved
by time,
        by tide,
to stone bowls,
        hollows,
Spring tide,
        at rising water's
    edge,
    a gift for the sea.

What is the taste of

a dream in the darkness?

How might you carry a dream?

In a pocket,

a cage or

a basket?

Tangled in memory,

twined round a heart?

Where would you keep it
for safety?

Can you lock up a dream,

with a key?

Or, should you trust

to the light

to keep a dream safe,

keep it close, keep it near?

What are the colours

             of dreaming?

Are they layered, like mist,

are they coloured, like gold

and fragile like fragments,

like leaves in the wind?

Do they long for the dark

           and the moon?

Does a dream find each
dreamer? Does it seek in
the night, searching for
someone who might understand
the why and the wherefore,
the warp and the weft?
Can you hunt for a dream
with a hound at your heels?

Can you hunt for a dream
with a hawk on your glove?
Must you search in silence,
in secret, in shadow?
Wait, watch and listen.
Between a breath and a breath
you might find a taste of a
dream in the dark. Never fear

River-light and
leaf-light, sunlight
and ripple – oak, beech and
alder, hazel, ash, holly and birch.
Wind in the tree tops and
birds in the branches.
And beech leaves
are faeries'
gold.

Walking,
I became entangled
in the songs of grasshoppers,
seduced by the scent of clover,
lulled by the warmth of the sun.
And birds,
always the language of birds.
Distance becomes measured
by the conversations of birds.

Heat coils in the lane

where adder sleeps.

In this moment he is

a still point of wild peace,

a pattern of sun and shade,

a warm, wild life.

Disturbed, he unwinds,

slides into shadow, is gone.

The space between each season -

Winter to spring; single swallows

signs of hope. Spring to summer;

blossom turns to fruit.

Summer to autumn; leaf gilds tree

and swallows sit, notes on wires.

Autumn to winter; berries blush

hawthorn trees red. Birds feast.

With courage
small spirit sings,
in the darkness
of the hedges,
from thorn,
from briar,

and her
small song
stitches
the heart
to the soul
with
music.

Ripple-light moves
over sea-smooth stone,

from the pool where
sandmartins dip from

sky to drink,
  to the sea where

the sea people swim,
cool fresh to salt
and rich with the
memory of water.

Finch flocks,

       feeding on seeds,

rise to the skies

       in a shower of song.

Swallows, low to the earth,

follow flight paths,

lines of old runways

       now fractured by flowers.

First steps into air, wings wide
to meet the current that lifts,
learning the pathways and patterns
of flight, then resting.
Bright eyed, cream breast, pale
blush crown, azure feathered back.
Fragile form, and yet how this
small-hearted creature weathers
fierce, wild storms.

In the space between

the edge of summer,

of autumn, late swallows,

martins, cross winged sky

with snipe, woodcock. Thorn

trees blush, red berry rich,

a waiting feast for fieldfare,

redwing, songthrush.

The winter acoustics

of a cold beach:

sound of the sea-smoothed

pebbles is softened by frost,

sand under foot cracks,

splinters with each step.

Whitesands Beach, January.

Stone keeps
company with
a woman of
gentle
heart and
spinners
skill, a
talisman.

See how,

     when letters join

together, how they dance across

a space like children,

    with hands linked.

     And isn't handwriting

simply the act of learning

the shapes of letters

    and drawing words.

Gold backed, black barred

the bee navigates

the thistled flowers of teasel.

Fragile petals fall

beneath her footfall.

A small shower of lilac.

A gift given on

on the beach at twilight, to

a woman who lived with a painter

A wild rabbit in the corner of

a green field.

Swallows, gathering on a wire.

A heron, flying low, passing

below the early morning sun.

Martins, dipping to drink

at a wind-splintered pond.

Cranefly wings, spider webs,

catching the light.

- warm air, and sunshine
- a clear river flowing over stone
- insect wings on summer days
- wind in the leaves of trees
- the colours of butterflies
- the brush of moth wings at night
- a nightingale
- the sound of dreams
- the shape of birds
- laughter, and forgetting
- the sound of rain
- the soft warmth of a curled cat
- and now, just to hold the hand
  of a friend, not seen for
  a while, and to be safe.

The texture of silence is

the absence of human,

enough breeze to hear

the leaf-song of trees,

small wings,

the conversations of birds.

How does it fall

that curlew call,

over river mouth

tidal-dark with silt?

Why does it pull

on the tide of the heart

as the moon pulls

at the heart of the sea?

Memory.

Feather,

found beneath trees,

resting on riverbank.

A wild sign,

talisman,

remembers the shape

of heron.

As the sea breathes in,

placed in a bowl

caved in the rock

by time,

by tide,

at the end of the day,

when the light gives way

to the beautiful darkness.

Winterwood

At the feet

of beech trees,

fallen leaves pattern the earth.

Fox-light,

red-gold,

glows bright,

colours the eyes with wild.

leaf

in hand

piece of

gold.

wish.

each

caught

a small

faeries'

a

Ice, formed at night

beneath a sky so clear,

and a moon a silver sliver,

and the perfect patterns

of planets and stars,

pinning the dark to the sky.

A sky so clear,

a river of stars and

hardly a moon and

winter's breath

holding water,

like stone, but,

ice carries the memory

of water.

The beautiful litter of

trees dances in the

ribbon-road that stretches

ahead and the sky is

rich with red kites.

Fallen leaves reveal the

subtle architecture of birds.

Tree gives

shade,

shelter,

warmth,

food,

beauty,

bounty,

breath.

Thoughts,

like leaves,

blown,

falling

                 almost

            impossible

      to catch, like wishes.

Hardly a breath, and yet

the leaves   danced

and the

beauty

of it

took

away

my breath

leaving only an understanding

Oak leaf
fallen and
leaves
litter

          quiet
          earth.
     Another season
swiftly turns.

There is a beauty to

the autumn hedges,

field edges,

where flocks of lapwing

brighten dark skies.

Autumn is a time for flocks,

starling, rook, jackdaw,

redwing.

In the absence

of the breath

of a breeze

leaves fall to earth.

A perfect circle

of bright gold

beneath the skeleton

of a tree.

Here,

at the edge of winter,

water has become glass.

Clear and clean,

it holds

the light.

For this moment

all is

At winter's edge,

water sharp as glass,

flowers push like spears

through frost-hard earth.

A fieldfare flies, feathers

bright, in a flock of

gold beaked blackbirds.

The peace of wild things.

Time flows like water.

Sometimes a river over rapids.

Sometimes locked in ice.

Sometimes spilling through

my open fingers even as

I try to cup, to hold, to stop,

time. It flows. Like water.

Do not feel caged

by bones. Roam beyond.

Reach for the raven.

Fly with finch flocks.

Rest in the earth with

drowsy adder, then rise

with larks on wings,

in song, and

become the leaves of trees

unfurling, falling.

Measure time by

the movement of the moon,

turning of the tide, and

understand that what

appears to be an ending

is only a change.

In from the sea

wind cool, sea deeper blue

than sky and the world

so empty of the sound of humans.

Stonecrop and heather fill soul
and land.

Let the wind take your troubles,

lift your heart, your spirit

and set your wild soul free.

51° 52' 31.92"N
5° 12' 54.03"W.
Minewells.

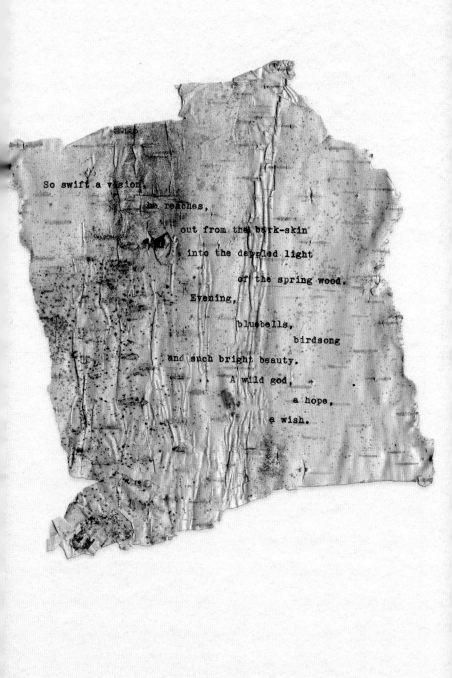

So swift a vision,

he reaches,

out from the bark-skin

into the dappled light

of the spring wood.

Evening,

bluebells,

birdsong

and such bright beauty.

A wild god,

a hope,

a wish.

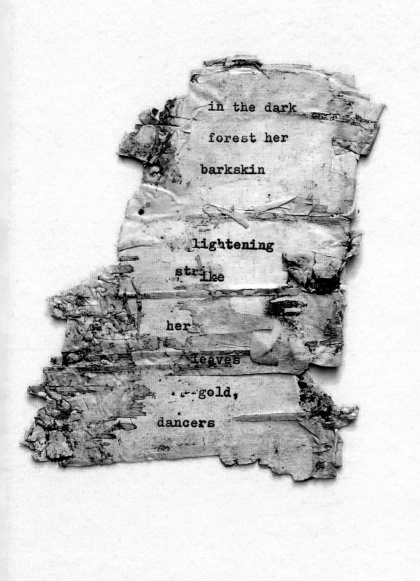

in the dark

forest her

barkskin

lightening

strike

her

leaves

gold,

dancers

She saw him once,
wild in the forest, he
peeled himself from the
silvered skin of a birch.
He was made from dark and
dappled leaf-light. From his
head branched antlers grew.
She knew then, even as the vision
of him faded, that they still lived,
the old ones, in the spaces between
the light and the dark, at the edge
of the wild, in the heart.

Autumn birch

is both

silver and

gold

Aspen
alive with light
and each leaf dances
with delight as the
year turns

Blue   Fallen

bar   feather

banded   found.

night sky   Sky litter,

evening   Banded memories

daybreak   jewel.

    Wild gift

Remnant of

     a charm,

they carry

     splinters

of sunlight,

     the memory

     of song.

Brush strokes of sepia,

barred and banded,

cuckoo is spring-bringer,

crossing continents

to call over heather,

heath and moorland,

from dawnlight to dusklight

and into the dark.

storm

beaten

lost

wild

litter

a

wild

gift of

half remembered

flight

after
the
storm,
remnants
of
Icarus.

even

now

feather

yearns

only

for

air

Too close to

the sun,

now frozen in time,

it was

never feathers

that failed me

in the high flight

to reach

for the stars.

She placed the

curse like a

web, falling

softly over each

of us, as we lay

sleeping.

How could   she know,

as bones became hollow

feathers broke through

skin, I would receive

her curse as a

blessing

when

feather

falls

does it

hold

in its veins

the memory

of   the world's

winds?

only in flight do we find freedom, joy and the peace of wild places

wild

blessing

Song of raven, the curlew's hymn

By feather, leaf, bark & stone

A leaf in water where otters swim

By feather, leaf, bark & stone

In sap that flows from root to crown

By feather, leaf, bark & stone

Shaped by tide's turn, smooth, round

By feather, leaf, bark & stone

Unbound is the world's first crowdfunding
publisher, established in 2011.

We believe that wonderful things can happen
when you clear a path for people who share
a passion. That's why we've built a platform
that brings together readers and authors
to crowdfund books they believe in –
and give fresh ideas that don't fit the
traditional mould the chance they deserve.

This book is in your hands because
readers made it possible.
Everyone who pledged their support
is listed on the following pages.
Join them by visiting unbound.com
and supporting a book today.

WITH SPECIAL THANKS

Anderida Books

Booka Bookshop

East Gate Bookshop

Era of Leek

Kenilworth Books

Masonville General Store

Poetry Pharmacy

Seven Fables Dulverton

The Bookery

The Little Book Emporium

UKBookworm

• A •

Hazel Abbott
Tamsin Abbott
Amira Abd El-Khalek
Violet Achilleos
Awkward Ada
Dave Adams
Jane Adams
Mary Jane Adams
David Adger
Shona Alexander
Ahlyah Ali
Katherine Alker
Wanda Allard
Christine Allen
Steph Allman
John Allum
Catherine Allwood
Peg Aloi
Simon Amers
Rebecca Amis
Petra Anders
Alison Anderson
Family Anderson
Melanie Anderson
Jane Angell
Sandra Armor
Catherine Arnold
Mary Aspinall
Suzanne Attree
Sandra Austin
James Aylett

• B •

Carole Backler
Karen Badenoch
Allison Bailey
Jackie Bailey
Joan Bailey
Lewis E Bailey
Duncan Baines
Anji Baker
Debby Baker
Ellie Baker
Suzan Baker
Lila Bakke
Deborah J Ballantyne
Jason Ballinger
Davina Balvack

Sara Jane Bankes @
BHAPottingSheds
Avril Banks
Leah Barabasz
Helen Barker
Andrew Barnebey
Pamela Barone
Janet Barraclough
Lucinda Barraclough
Chris Bartlett
Jon Bartlett
Sally Basile
Helen Bates
Catty Bateson
Margaret Bateson-Hill
Laura Baxter
Emma Bayliss
Darren Beadle
Chantelle Beagley
S Beale
Anna Bear
Michelle Bear
Clea Beasley
Paula Beasley
Kathy Beber
Amy-Jane Beer
Branimira Belegova
Carol Bell
Julie Bell
Lucy Bell
Megan Bell
Ronnie Bendall
Elizabeth Benjamin
Marianne Bennett
Dr. Mary Berry
Heidi Berthiaume
Nikki Bi
Heather Binsch
Lisa Sara Bird
Valerie and Julie Bishop
Carrie-Ann Black
Sarah Blenkinsop
Hannah Blunt
Lynne Bly
Nicki Bodenham
Denise Boggs
Gilly Bolton
Rachel Bond
Sara Booth
Helen Bosher
Karl Bovenizer

Stephen Bowden
Ann Bowen
Dorothy Bowen
Jo Bowen
Luke Bowyer
Vivien Boyes
Helen Bradshaw
Meri Brady
Jane Branson
Magalie Briand
Karen Bright
Gemma Bristow
Fran Broady
Dr Ruth Brompton-
Charlesworth
Nadine Brown
Pauline Brown
Zoe Brown
Lissa Brubaker
Amber Bruce
Catherine S Bruce
Matt Bruce
Melanie Bruce
Jane Brumwell
Erica Bullivant
Jendy Bullman
Susanna Bullman
Andrea Burden
Xanthe Phoebe Lily
Burdett
Stephanie Burgis
Ailbhe Burke
Bonnie Ann Burnett
Sam Burns
Sara Burns
Etho Burrow
Janina Byrne

• C •

Corin Caliendo
Fiona M H Campbell
Jane Campbell
Trish Campbell
Valerie Campbell
Melanie Cannon
Jennie Cappleman
Victoria Capps
Elizabeth Card
Maddie Carey
Melissa Carey

Anne Carlile
Caitriona Carlin
Ruth Carter
Wendy Carter
Holly Cartlidge
Hazel Chadwick
Mia Chadwick
Lisa Chaffer
Barbara Challender
Caroline Champin
Helen Champion
Emily Chaplin
John Luke Chapman
Thalia Charles
Elizabeth Charlesworth
Richard Charlesworth
Lindsay Chase
Choy Cheam-Sheikh
Lucy Chessum
Daniel Chisham
Khadim Chishti
Samantha Chorley
Angela Christian
Linda Church
Fi Clark
Rachel Clarke
Louisa Clarkson
Sam Clayton
Jenna Clements
Do Cleworth
Cadi Cliff
Gill Clifford
Freyalyn Close-
Hainsworth
Tracey Clough
Eileen Coates
Lucy Coats
Larri Cochran
GMark Cole
Kate Coleman
Toria Collins
Anastasia Colman
Emily Comyn
Dom Conlon
Sarah Connor
Deborah Conway Read
Jude Cook
Leah Cooke
Bethan Coombs
Denise Cooper
Sheryl Cooper

Gillian Cornwall
Andrew Correia
Teresa Cotterell
Bob Cotterill
Carin Couch Loy
Shelley Coulter-Smith
SJ Cowell
Geoff Cox
June & Gerry Craddock
Wendy Craig
Tina & Mike Crawley
Stephanie Crewes
Melissa Crocker
Sophie Crofts
Julia Croyden
Pat Cruse
Kevin Culling
Kristofer Cullum-
Fernandez
Mandy Curnock

• D •

Robina D'Arcy-Fox
Adam D'Souza
Sue Dabner
Jane Dallaway
Emma Daly
Danielle M. Dani
Liz Daniels
Lorijo Daniels
Elizabeth Darracott
Eileen Davidson
Amy Davies
Andrea Davies
Bev Davies
Cathy Davies
Emma Davies
Harriet Fear Davies
Helena Davies
Nicola Davies
Claire Davies & Chris
Goodwin
Hilary Davis
Laura Davis
Patricia Davis
Rosa Davis
Stephanie Davis
Kate Dawson
Isabella Day
Scott Day

Marianne De Giovanni
Christiaan de Haes
Sarah Deakin
Debbie Dean
Katherine Dearness
Ash Demetriou
Valerie Demouy
Anne Deneen
Miranda Denison-Lowe
Allison Dennis
Nicola Dennis
Beth Deuble
Annette Dewgarde
Sunny-Blue DeWilde
Cathy Dixon
Nicola Dodd
Erica Donner
Mary Alice Dooley
Amanda-Jane Doran
Marina Dorward
Linda Doughty
Cressida Downing
Alex Doyle
Jill Doyle
Ros Draper
Donna Drouin
Rebekah Drury
Allan Dryer
David Dubbert
Tracy Duddridge
Anne Dunn
Val Duskin
Ellie-May Dwyer

• E •

Samantha Easter
Lisa Ecclestone
Rags Edward
Josie Edwards
Rachel Edwards
Cecibel Egan-Huamán
Tywysoges Eira
Esther Ellen
Marti Eller
Karin Elliott
Cherie Ellis
Gita Engelen
Pascale F. Engelmajer
Elisabeth England
Anna Ermakova

Monty Erskine
Lauren Eunson
Amanda Evans
Cath Evans
Catherine Evans
Gillian Evans
Judy Evans
Lucy Everett
Kateri Ewing
Emma Exelby
Jackie Eyers

• F •

Chris Facer
Sylvia Fagetti
Angela Fahy
Rachel Fairbank
Trish Fairbeard
May Fairweather
Neil Fallon
Emma Farey
Kay Farmer
Suzanne Farmer
Lisa Lea Faught
Hannah Fazakerley
Fiona Feather
Allison Felmy
Lorna Fergusson
Cam Field
Kandyce Fillmore
Ed Finch
Eden Finch
Fiona Finch
Samantha Finlay
Fiona
Cathy Fisher
Matt Fisher
Cara Fitzmaurice
Helena Flowers
Jane Flynn
Helen Foley
Phyl Foley
Joanna Forbes
Lynne Ford
Helen Forshaw
Karen Forshaw
Laura Fox
Sally Ann Fox
Roz Fox-Bentley
Gillian Foxcroft

John Francis
Philippa Francis
Julian Francis-Lawton
Chris Fraser
Delphine Fraser
Shona Fraser
Christine Freeman
Sara Freid
Kathleen Friend
Jennie Fytche

• G •

Georgia Gałus
Barbara Ganley
Ian Gardiner
Mary Garland
Russell Geake
Jeannine Gehrmann
James George
Chris Gerrard
Amelia Gersema
Dan Gibson
Lyn Gibson
Julie Giles
Shonagh Giles
Jane Gill
Mhairi Gillen
Melanie Gillespie
Barbara Gittes
Steve Gladwin
Juliana Glanfield
Vivien Gledhill
Jo Glen
Jude Glendinning
Vernon Goddard
Anne Goldsmith
Elizabeth Gooch
Lynne Goodacre
Laura Goodfellow
Stacy Gormley
Sonia Goulding
Elizabeth Gradie
Lynda Graves
Janet Gray
Simon Gray
Stephanie Grayling
Rosie Green
Elaine Greene
Phil Greenland
Susanne Griffin

Karen Griffiths
Claire Grinham
Olga D Grovic
Renee Guillory
Philippa Gurney
Agnes Guyon

• H •

Mary H.
Terri Stewart Hackler
Kathrine Haddrell
Cheryl Hagen
Kristine Haig
Gemma Hale
Amanda Hall
Kim Hall
Dorothy Hallam
Rennie Halstead
Sophia Hanifah
Hilary Harley
Candy Harman
Jac Harmon
Emily Ruth Harris
Neil Harris Tily
Eve Harrison
Tim Harwood
Jackie Hassine
Wendy Havelock
Dominique Hawksley
Leti Hawthorn
Tracy Hayes
Cate Haynes
Caroline Hayward
Elspeth Head
Andrew Hearse
Gillian Heaslip
Rebecca Heaton
Koreen Heaver
Becca Heavrin
Sharon Heels
Sherry Helwer
Joshua Heming
Vicky Hempstead
Helen Hennerley
Audrey Hetherington
Cecilia & Graham
Hewett
Gail Hewitt
Gwyneth Hibbett
Jane Hill

Joan Hill
Kathryn Hill
Lyn Hill
Stuart Hill
Charlotte Hills
Michael Hines-Mackay
Natasha Hobday
Sue Hodgetts
Ann Hodgson
Lisa Hofmann
Gemma Holden
Jackee Holder
Laura Holland
Helen Holman
Gilly Holmes
Lisa Holmes
Nikki Holmes
Katie Holten
Denise Davis Homer
Sue Homer
Jacob Hope
Steph Hope
Beth Hopkins
Elizabeth Hopkinson
Avril Horn
Xenia Horne
Angharad Horsey
Matthew Horsham
Eric Horstman
Sue House
Susan Housley
Anna Houston
Jo Howard
Julia Howell-Cortelli
Antonia Hoyle
Kath Hudson
Joe Huggins & Kimberly
Pugliese
Bethan Hughes
Hilary Hughes
Richard Hughes
Elizabeth Humphreys
Allison Hunter Hill
Tasneem Zehra Husain
Liz Hyder

• I •

Elizabeth Irvine
Ann Ishiguro

• J •

Dee Jackson
Kimberly Jackson
Melanie Jackson
Shani Jackson
Rachel Jaffe
Alison James
Ally James
Rene' Janiece
Lizzie Jarvis
Kay Jay
Jeannie
Dan Jenkins
Jenn
Lynds Jennings
Christine Jensen
Eva John
H C Johnson
Kathryn Johnson
Laurel Johnson
Laurie Johnson
Michele Johnson
Simon Johnson
Zoë Johnson
Michelle Johnson-
Weider
Cathy Johnston
Bodhi Jon
Casey Jon
Cathy Jones
Kathy Jones
Laura Jones
Michael Jones
Sue Jones
Truus Joosten
Mary Jordan-Smith
Caroline Jorna
Mary Jowitt
Erin Julian
Genevieve Jung
Karen Jurgens

• K •

Olya K-Mehri
Axel Kacoutié
Kathlyn
Brienne Keigwin
Debbie Kelly
Lizzie Kempton

Tony Kendle
C Louise Kennedy
Jane Kenneway
Rhiannon Kennion
Ali Kenny
Aaron Kent
Helen Kent
Rebecca Kershaw
Ruth Keys
Mobeena Khan
Dan Kieran
Jill Kieran
Caitlin Kight
Aly Kimber-Herridge
Ingrid Kincaid
Eleanor King
Ellia King
June Kingsbury
Liz Kirby
Olaf Kirch
Stephen Kirk
Jackie Kirkham
Kerry Kittrell, The
Cauldron Crone
Nichola Knight
Tessa Knight
Mitzi Koch
Mary Jo Koehler
Rebecca Kohn
Dawn Kozoboli
Elise Kress
Jane Lembeck Kuesel
Giovanna Kuwertz

• L •

Sheryl Labouchardiere
Hamish Laing
Ann Lally
Jen Lamb
Jon Lambert
Julie Laming
Reni Landor
Angela Lane
Matt Larsen-Daw
Phil Latham
Liz Latto
Sarah K Lawson
Freya Marie Lawton
Alison Layland
Lind

Amy Lee
Caroline Lee
Evalyn Lee
Emma Legge
Benedict Leigh
Malcolm Leith
Carol Lenox
Anouska Lester
Bethan Lewis
Catherine Lewis
Diane Lewis
Kirsty Lewis
Maria Jessica Lewis
Alison Leyland
Patrick Limb
Lind
Maggie Lindsay
Rachel Lindsay
Cathy Llewellyn
Jo Lloyd
Patricia Ann Salazar
Lloyd
Heidi Logie
Gillian Lonergan
Nancy Baldwin Long
Diana Longworth
Chris Loughran
Racheblue Love
Wendy Love Hinds
Elizabeth Lovegrove
Lisa Lovett
Sophie Lovett
Catriona M. Low
Alison Lowe
Brigid Lowe
Janet Loy
Bea Lubbers
Mezzie Elen Lucerne-
Lambourne
Brian Lunn
Jen Lunn
Patterson Lyles
Zoe Lynch
Sadaf Lynes
Yvonne Lyon

• M •

Calum Macaulay
Dianne MacDonald

Megan MacGregor
Anu MacIntosh-Murray
Sarah MacLachlan
Rhona MacLennan
Finlay MacLeod
Tracey MacLeod
Sheila MacNeill
Kirstie Macqueen
Sarah Maguire
Sonia Mainstone-Cotton
Carmeletta Malora
Philippa Manasseh
Lizzie Mann of Canada
David Manns
Judy Mansfield
Sarah Manton
Oileàn Mara
Linda Marchisotto
Naomi Markham
Penny Marsden
Shelley Marsden
Lorie Marsh
Mary Martes
Jill Martin
Stacie Margaret Martin
Amanda Masterson
Indigo Maughn
Betsy Maxwell
Emily Maycock
Marta McCabe
Bridget Rose McCall
George McCallum
Yvonne Carol
McCombie
Noelle McCormack
Rebecca McCredie
Phyllis McDaniel
Elizabeth McEvoy
Fiona McGavin
Julie McGregor
Lauren McGregor
Holly McGuigan
Sharon McHale
Marian McHugh
Susan McKenzie
Caitlin McKiernan
Graham McLachlan
Sue Yin McMahon
Hettie McNeil
Katie McNeil

Jennie McNeill
Rita Meehan
Mary Megarry
Catherine Meldrum
Ian Mella
Catherine Melser
Pearl Melvill
Lisa Mersky
Kristina Meschi
Ivana Mestrovic
Meg Middleton
Susan Middleton
Kizzia Mildmay
Belle Miles
Jenny Miles
Sarah Miles
Kathryn Milford
Tracey Millar
Brittany Miller
Hope Miller
Debs Mills
John Mitchinson
David Mizon
James Moakes
Alison Mold
Sheilagh Molloy
Be Montague
Ann Montgomery
Crystal Moore
Hedda Moore
Sheela Moorthy
Becky Moreton
Margaret Morgan
Rosie Bess Morgan
Suzanne Morgan
Jayne Morrisey
Conifer Morze
Roxanne Eleanor Wren
Moss
Martha Mountain
Mouse
Bernard Moxham
Alison Mudd
Kim Mullen-Kuehl
Catherine Mullis
Willow Murphy
Gus and Julie Murray
Peter Murray
Jennifer Muscato
Kirsten Muzeen

• N •

Nadine
Stu Nathan
Carlo Navato
Jayne Neal
Jackie Needham
Jacqui Newberry
John Newbold
Amy Newman
Penny Newns
Haulwen Nicholas
Helen Nicholas
Julie Nicholson
Josh Niesse
Gwendolyn Noble
Ariel Noffke
Evelyn Norris
Ems Norton

• O •

Colleen O'Brien
Ruth O'Leary
Rachel O'Meara
Karen O'Sullivan
Amanda O'Dwyer
Elizabeth O'Grady
Patricia Oakley
Julie Oates
Saranne Oberman
Elizabeth OBrien
Helen Oliver
Ingrid Oomen
Angela Osborne
Jay Osborne
Christine Overend
Julia Owen
Paula Owen

• P •

Laurie Pachter
Ryan S. Padnuk
Michelle Padula
Paula Page
Eileen Palmer
Vicki Palmer
Paula Palyga
Yi Pang

Katharine Parker
Kate Parsons
Trish Paton
Adam Ross Patterson
Donna Pauley
Carol L Peachee
Esme Pears
Jane Pearson
Robert Pearson
Liz Pearson Mann
Cal Peck
Erik & Jocelyn Pedersen
Rosie Pendlebury
Ashleigh Pepper-Bowen
Helen Perkins
Catherine Perlich
Lesley Peters
Mags Phelan Stones
Karen Phillips
Liz Phillips
Nise Phillips
Lizzie Pickering
Catherine Pickersgill
Katharine Pickup
Karen F. Pierce
Sophie Pierce
Kathy Piotter
Linda Pippin
Ameena Ahsan Pirbhai
Karen Plested
Kate Plews
Anne Plowright
Dinny Pocock
Sarah Poland
Pamela Polbaciu
Justin Pollard
Bridget Poole
Jenny Pope
Victoria Pope
Dion Potter
Tara Prayag
Rebecca Prentice
Janet Pretty
Popi Pribojac
Brenda Elizabeth Price
Malcolm Prue
Karen Puffett
Sarah Pugh
Adele Pugsley
Claire Pulford

Eileen Pun
Shanee Puri
Sue Purkiss

• Q •

Kitti Quarfoot
Lisa Quattromini
Lisa Quelcuti
Eimear Quigley
Lynn Quinn
Eva Quiñones
Meabh Quoirin

• R •

Iulia Racovita
Sunita Rajakumar
Christine Raquez
Beverly Raskin
Fiona Razvi
Ailke Shira Rechenberg
Alison Rees
Ffion Rees
Amelia Regan
Jane Reid
Lara Reid
Betty Rembert
Cornelia Rémi
Nicola Joy Rennie
Gordon Rice
Alison Richardson
Julie Ridley
Sarah Rigby
Laing Rikkers
Katya Riley
Sonia Ritter
Jemima Rivers
Gareth Roberts
Julie Roberts
Kristina Roberts
Rachel Roberts
Terry Robertson
Donald Robertson-
Adams
Mark Robinson
Laura Robson Brown
Satya Robyn
Bernadette Rodbourn
Rachael Rodway

Lorraine Rogerson
Alice Rohdich
Barbara Roidl
Robyn Roscoe
Julie Rose
Kalina Rose
Tamsin Rosewell
Becks Rossiter
Rhona Rowland
Sarah Royston
Sarah Rudder
Lydia Ruffin
Emine Rushton
Fiona Russell
Joni Russell
Katherine Russell
Lynn Russell
Susan Rutherford

• S •

Mary Sadler
Anita Sams
Sandra
Diana Santos
Lyni Sargent
Claire Sauer
Kat Savage
Janet Scherczer
Sue Schnabel
Roz Schneider
Amanda Schreier
Svenia Schreiner
Janette Schubert
Barbara Schwartzbach
Debra Schwyhart
Matthew Scott
Jori Scruggs-Brown
Kate Scuffle
Esme Segerberg
Karen Selley
Shayna Sessler
Tanya Shadrick
Deborah Blackburn
Shakotko
Robin Shambach
Harriet Shannon
Maggie Sharps
Alison Shaw
Fiona Shaw

Karen Shaw
Marnie Shaw
Laura Sheldon
G C O Shelford
Jacqueline & Francis
Shepherd
Tina Shewring
Graeme Shilland
Andrea Shinton
The Shipley Family
Debbie Shore
Jo Ellen Shumway
Sharon Shute
Robert Siegle
Margaret & Roy Simons
Erin Kathleen Simpson
Isabel Sinagola
Sally Sines
Udaybhanu Sinh
Lindsay Skudder
Debbie Slaterx
Caroline Slough
Darryl Smart
Catherine Smillie
Maxine Smillie
Carolyn Smith
Lorraine Smith
Penelope Smith
Sarah Smith
John Smithies
Sjoera Snijder-Sahuleka
Murielle Solheim
Jo Solliday
Faye Somerville
Alison Souter
Kit Spahr
Stephen Sparks
Mary Helen Speir
Anna Spencer
Beverly Spencer
Tessa Spencer
Karen Spy
Teresa Squires
Wendy Staden
Marketa Stafkova
Ruthie Starling
Brenda Steel
Cate Steele
Shirley Steer
Giulia Stefan & Mick

Heffernan
Gabriela Steinke
Robin Stenham
Kathryn Stephenson
Linda Sterrett-Marple
Gemma Stevens
Linda Stevens
Ruth Stevens
Jan Stevenson
Dr Catriona Stewart
OBE
Pamela Marion Stewart
Watson
Lisa Stockley
Aurora Stone
Corinne Stone
Gwilym Stone
Gavin Francis
Stoneystreet
Ellen Stratton
Brigit Strawbridge
Yasmin Strube
Susan Stuart
Jet Stukey
Sue Sturtevant
Lesley Styles
Arthi Subramanian
Rajeevi Subramanian
Sue Sullivan
Mary Swainson
Kaola Swanson
Shanti Syal
Alison Sykes
Romey Sylvester
Paula Symonds
Dora Szuromi

• T •

Catherine Tagg
Emily Jane Tamas
Abigail Taylor
Fiona Taylor
Fiona A W Taylor
Georgette Taylor
Laura Taylor
Lorna Taylor
Lorraine Taylor
Paul Taylor
Abbe Taylor-Billington

Liz Tears
Roger ter Haar
Deborah Texeira
Penny Thomas
Brewer Thompson
David Thompson
Helen Thompson
Liz Thompson
Pen Thompson
Jo Thompson Coon
Roger Thorp
Bec Tigue
Adam Tinworth
Lucy Tipper
Kathryn Tipping
Heather Tisdale
Professor Karen Tocque
Eileen Todd
Narisa Togo
Pippa Tolfts
Lou Tonkin
Artemis Toouli
Sabine Tötemeyer
Jeni Toth
Fiona Tough
Angela Townsend
Helen Treml
Jonathan Treml
Louise Treneman
Jan Trenoweth
Lindsay Trevarthen
Sarah Trew
Jayne Truran
Chloe Truslove
Hazel Tufton
Lewis Turner
Curzon Tussaud
Rosie Tuszynska
Jessica Twyman
Becky Tyler-Rickon
I. Tyler-Rickon
Simon Tyrrell
Vangelis Tzanatos

• U •

Wendy Uchimura
Janet Ulman
Caroline Underwood
Michelle Underwood

Clive Upton
Keith & Gill Urry
Jennifer Uzzell

• V •

Jo Valentine
Sas(kia van der sluis) of
Amsterdam
Lies Vanhoucke
Christine Vassie
Mark Vent
Annaleen Vermeulen
Linda Verstraten &
Pyter Wagenaar
Debbie Voller
Sabine Voßkamp
Georgina Vye

• W •

Dianna W
Julie Walden
Finlay Walkden
Genevieve Walker
Martin John Walker
Catherine Walker
McKinney
Jamie Wallace
Claire Walsh
Matthew Walsh
Ali Walters
Alison Walters
Sandy Walther
Wendy-Jane Walton
Ellen Waters
Julie Watkins
Anna Watson
Laura Alice Watt
Chris Watts
Paul & Ann Watts
Amanda Wearing
E Webb
Patricia Welsh
Lorien Wendt
Angharad Westmore
Katie Weston
Luke Weston
Orla Whalley
Katy Wheatley

Jennifer Whitbread
Georgina White
Vennie Eline White
White Bear Woman
Miranda Whiting
Hatti Whitman
Patty Whitney
MaryRuth Wiggins
Claire Williams
David Williams
Debra Jeremy Harri &
Efan Williams
Jacqueline Williams
Philippa Williams
Rosemary Williams
Pauline Williams and
Mel Bale
Chris Willis
Sean Wilson
Jeff Wince
Rosie Winyard
Nastassja Wiseman
Sharon Witt
Rachel Wood
Cathy Wood and Evie
Mercia
Lea Woodlands
Rebecca Woodward
Alexandra Worth
Laura Wreschnig
Donna Wright
Michelle Wright
Marieke Wrigley
Jo Wylderidge

• Y •

Lisa Yallamas
Sharon Yates
Zoë Yates
Arisa Yoshida
Angela Young
Rick Young
Stephanie Young

• Z •

Tad Zaranko
Natalia Zukerman

First published in 2022

Unbound
Level 1, Devonshire House, One Mayfair Place, London W1J 8AJ
www.unbound.com

"How Surely Gravity's Law" by Rainer Maria Rilke is taken from
Rilke's Book of Hours, translation copyright © Anita Barrows and
Joanna Macy, 1996. Used by permission of Riverhead, an imprint of
Penguin Publishing Group, a division of Penguin Random House LLC.

Design by Alison O'Toole

A CIP record for this book is available from the British Library

ISBN 978-1-80018-155-7 (trade hbk)
ISBN 978-1-80018-195-3 (limited edition)

Printed in Italy by L.E.G.O SpA

3 5 7 9 8 6 4 2